AF256917

Robert's Rules of Order

A Complete Guide to Robert's Rules of Order

Table of Contents

Introduction

Thank you for taking the time to pick up this book about Robert's Rules of Order.

Robert's Rules were first established in 1863 as a way to better assist in bringing efficiency, legitimacy, fairness, uniformity and competence to the way meetings ran among Army personnel. Since that time, Robert's Rules have been updated and expanded upon, and are now used in organizations of all types and sizes.

This book covers the topic of Robert's Rules and how to understand and implement them yourself. In the following chapters you will learn of the different Rules of Order you must follow, as well as the definitions of many terms used within Robert's Rules.

Finally, you will be provided with strategies as to how you may introduce Robert's Rules to your specific organization, be it a company, charity, sporting club, sorority, or otherwise!

Once again, thanks for choosing this book, I hope you find it to be helpful!

Chapter 1: History and Use of Robert's Rules

We have all experienced one of those dreaded business meetings that seem to drag on with one person doing all the talking. Perhaps, if we have not had that experience, instead it was one of those club get-togethers when the very outspoken person pushed to build a pool outside the clubhouse that your club really did not have the funds to build. Maybe, in fact, you were simply hanging out with friends and you noticed that one of the more soft-spoken of your group, maybe even you, did not get a chance to suggest where to eat for his or her own birthday.

Robert's Rules of Order grew out of a need for efficiency, a desire for legitimacy, a hope for fairness, and a simple striving for uniformity and competence in running meetings across the United States. It started with Henry Martyn Robert, an Army officer of civil engineering in 1863, when Robert was 26 years old. Leaders of a public community meeting held in a church setting asked Robert to preside over the gathering. Robert had never attempted anything like it before, and it seems that, in Robert's mind at least, the results were disastrous.

Robert searched out and studied the few books he could find concerning *parliamentary law*, the rules and guidelines for running parliamentary bodies and decision-making teams. Later the Army transferred him to San Francisco, and Robert discovered a complete non-uniformity in how the Army meetings were run across the United States, not to mention how meetings outside the Army functioned.

Determined to assist in bringing efficiency, legitimacy, fairness, uniformity and competence to the way meetings ran among Army personnel and throughout the nation, Robert compiled a book of common parliamentary law known as *Robert's Rules of Order*, though the official title was *Pocket Manual of Rules of Order for Deliberative Assemblies*. Eventually, Robert was promoted to General in the Army and his *Rules of Order* became the official text for a great majority of assemblies and meetings.

Throughout the years, there have been two revisions and ten additional editions, with General Robert's heirs very much involved in the updating and revisions. The latest edition is called *Robert's Rules of Order Newly Revised* and is the Eleventh Edition of the work. Generally, people consider Robert's Rules to be *the* parliamentary authority and look to his *Rules of Order* in matters of deliberative process.

Who Uses Robert's Rules?

Any group that must come to a decision can use Robert's Rules, though generally they are used by deliberative or parliamentary assemblies, that is, but formal groups of people who come together on a regular basis concerning a specific cause or topic. Often one of our first inclinations is to associate parliamentary process with law-making assemblies like the House of Representatives and the Senate. Indeed, the process that the House runs influenced *Robert's Rules* fundamentally and they are very applicable to government assemblies and community and city councils.

The corporate world can also benefit greatly from the use of *Robert's Rules* as a means of organizing meeting procedures. In addition, organizations without as much concern for turning a profit have something to gain from these parliamentary rules as well. Organizations such as fraternities, sports leagues, church groups, school boards, hobby clubs, scientific organizations, gaming clubs, volunteer organizations, teachers' associations, student governments, and cultural groups, along with a myriad of other types of associations and groups, would find *Robert's Rules* helpful if they were to adopt even just some of them.

Benefits of Adopting Robert's Rules

The Rules that Robert put forth in his book have many benefits. First, instituting Robert's Rules sets an expectation within an assembly of people as to how they will act. Such expectations are agreed upon by the assembly, so holding those who agreed to the bylaws accountable becomes less awkward and more natural. If the vote is to adopt Robert's Rules, then people will feel a sense of order and predictability, lending them the safety of a framework within which they can put forward their ideas for consideration.

Closely tied into this sense of safety is the right of every member, of both the minority and the majority, the absent and the present, to be heard. This system of deliberation respects every group, sub-group, and individual while making the best decision for the group as a whole.

Adopting Robert's Rules will also allow everyone to share a language of deliberation so that everyone speaks with the same terminology, reducing confusion and embarrassment as well as avoiding any awkwardness. This helps people understand what to expect from themselves and others.

Robert's Rules require a record of minutes, too, which creates accountability of the assembly and of the members to accomplish what they have voted to accomplish. This helps avoid legal trouble as well, as the group votes on accepting the minutes from the last gathering and deliberates upon any corrections, making the entire group accountable to each other as well as to the written word.

Finally, one of the main purposes of Robert's Rules was to make processes of decision-making more efficient. This is accomplished through various means, such as limits on speaking times, and having and abiding by a preset agenda.

Some Gentle Precautions

When you adopt Robert' Rules, you have a lot of flexibility in relaxing the rules, though of course you can use them "out of the box," the way they are written, as well. Robert's Rules are as helpful and efficient or as invasive and awkward as you make them.

One way to ensure that your adoption of Robert's Rules is as smooth as possible is to ensure that every member of the parliamentary body is offered access to a copy of the rules and written by-laws of the organization. Encourage your members to read with the intention to use the rules, and also assure them that practice will help with understanding. Create a forgiving and graceful environment because the learning curve will be different for everyone.

Another important expectation you must set is that this process might not meet the needs of *every* individual, but rather of the group as a whole. On the other hand, it *will* allow every member the opportunity to be heard, and these rules will protect that privilege.

Finally, be prepared to deal with those who might use the parliamentary process to their own selfish advantage. It is a somewhat common complaint that certain individuals will take advantage of others' lack of understanding of the process to squelch the voice of those with whom they disagree. You must prepare yourself with knowledge and firm grace to address this person's misuse of Robert's Rules.

These challenges to implementing Robert's Rules might seem a bit overwhelming, but they will be well worth the trouble. They will make your meetings much more efficient, fair, and even enjoyable.

Chapter 2: The Basics of Parliamentary Process

Before we look at the specifics of Robert's Rules, it is important to understand the terminology and guiding principles. In this chapter you will find some basic key terms, as well as gain an understanding of the driving forces behind parliamentary law. You will find more key terms scattered throughout the book in bold italics. Their definitions accompany them.

Some Key Terms

An ***assembly***, otherwise known as a "deliberative assembly," is the name for the group of members of an organization.

A ***member*** is an individual who belongs to an organization and who possesses the right to vote and deliberate along with other members to make decisions for the organization as a whole.

An ***officer*** is an individual, often chosen from the membership, who is elected to lead the members in some aspect of parliamentary procedure.

Parliamentary procedure is another name for the rules by which a meeting of members and officers functions.

A ***meeting*** is a gathering of enough members and officers to establish a ***quorum***, the minimum number needed to be present for a meeting. In a meeting, topics related to the activities of an organization are discussed, or deliberated upon, and decisions are made based on these discussions.

A ***motion*** is how a meeting moves forward. Members make motions, or proposals, which are then voted upon and adopted or rejected, and by these motions the discussion is propelled forward.

The ***presiding officer***, otherwise known as the president or chairman, leads the meeting by taking motions and putting them before the assembly for a vote, or by deciding upon them on his or her own.

A **bylaw** is a rule written "in stone," per se, that guides and limits all parliamentary proceedings within the assembly.

Democratic Principles

The basic process of parliamentarian assemblies is based on democratic principles. When an organization is committed to democratic values and the democratic process, the following are true of it:

1) The members vote is the decision-making process by which they rule in the organization. The vote dictates the outcome of deliberation.

2) Ideas that are presented to the assembly originate with members of the assembly.

3) Leaders are of the people and chosen by vote, or through election by the people.

4) There exist checks and balances between the members and the leadership of the assembly that is established by the governing charter or documents and upheld by the accountability of the assembly.

5) Each and every member is counted as equal, both in rights and in responsibilities.

6) In the spirit of democracy and following from the equality of the members, the entire assembly and meeting is run with fairness and based on impartiality. Agreed-upon laws and rules run the organization, not the fallible human leadership.

7) Each member is entitled to equal justice under the organization's laws. This mostly applies to the

removing and replacing of officers, such that the officers (as well as members) have a right to a fair trial under the law of the organization.

8) The majority vote rules the organization, yet the minority's and the absent members' rights are protected under the law of a democratic assembly such that all members have equal information and ability to speak.

9) The entire meeting and conduct of the organization is based in openness rather than in a spirit of secrecy. Notes, meetings, records, minutes, reports and notices are all available for inspection by the members.

10) Members possess the right to resign. Officers can resign from office and members can resign from the organization of their own purposes an accord, and are not tied to their office or membership by the rest of the membership.

Parliamentary process is then defined within these boundaries of democratic ideas. The process of deliberative assemblies is then based on three guiding principles, which can be further broken down into secondary guidelines and rules.

The Three Principles of Parliamentary Process

The first guiding principle is that business must be taken up one item at a time. As a result:

1) Everything in a meeting is taken in order of the predetermined agenda. This is the order of business.

2) There is allowed only one main motion to be pending at a time.

3) Resulting from the previous rule that only one motion may be pending at a time, members of the assembly can make secondary motions, which will be explained later in this book.

4) Only one member of the deliberation team may have the floor at any point in time. This is to protect the right of any and every member to be heard.

5) Following from the previous rule, members must take turns to speak.

6) To protect the assembly from being dominated by a single member or group, no member can speak twice about a single motion until every member of the assembly has had the opportunity to speak once first.

The second guiding principle promotes courtesy and respect among the members of an assembly, as well as protects justice, impartiality, and equality.

As a result:

1) The person presiding over the meeting will call the meeting to order at the time which it was scheduled.

2) Conversation stops and the members of the group take their seats promptly as soon as the meeting is called to order.

3) The members that are giving reports are seated at the front during the meeting.

4) Members of the assembly stand up to be recognized by the officer presiding and do not speak at inappropriate times or out of turn.

5) Members refer to each other and to the chairperson and officers in the third person, using, for example, "Madam Chairman," "the previous

speaker," and "the delegate from Orange County," and using the pronouns, "he" and "she."

6) Throughout the deliberation process, delegates refer to each other through the chair or presiding officer, never cross-talking directly to each other but rather channeling every comment through the office that is presiding.

7) Members respect each other by avoiding talk of others' motives or personalities, but instead focusing solely on the motion in order.

8) The presiding officer addresses members in third person as well, especially when correcting one of them or a group of them.

9) The assembly members speak with a clear, loud voice for all to hear.

10) The assembly members listen quietly while another member, officer, or the presiding officer is speaking.

Additionally:

11) The presiding officer does not side with either party in the debate, but allows both to be heard impartially and equally.

12) The presiding officer as well as the members ought to be aware of these rules and apply them.

13) The presiding officer carries the responsibility to make sure that the rules of debate are abided and that the various sides of an issue are equally heard.

14) Members may and have the right to ask to vote by ballot to protect their own and others' privacy. This is especially applicable during a controversial issue.

15) When a member is accused of wrongdoing or charged with an offense, the member has a right to a fair trial.

Finally, there is the rule of the majority while protecting the rights of the minority that plays a crucial role in shaping the parliamentary process. This rule is kept in place by a few guidelines as follows:

1) Members possess the right to receive notice for every meeting, though there exist various ways in which this notice can be sent: electronically, by post, by phone, by informing members at a previous meeting, etc.

2) Members possess the right to be informed by previous notice when something previously adopted is up for rescinding or amending.

3) Anytime a right or rights might be withdrawn from members, a two-thirds vote rather than a majority vote is required to pass the motion and approve it instead of the majority.

4) There is no time at which someone may require more than a majority vote on an issue or motion unless the bylaws or the authority on parliamentary process that is in use requires as such.

5) Members possess the right to hear and be informed about the work of the organization or assembly of which they are a part. This includes the reading of minutes and the reports by officers of actions (and the consequences thereof) taken by the organization.

Chapter 3: Running a Meeting

Now that we understand some of the philosophies and principals behind parliamentarian processes, let us take a look at the process itself.

The Order of Business

The order of business is generally accepted to be as follows:

1) The secretary or other officer reads the minutes from the last meeting and the assembly approves them.

2) Officers, boards, and standing committees give their reports and the assembly discusses them.

3) Special committees give their reports.

4) Special orders, such as motions postponed and voted to become special orders by two-thirds vote and once-yearly business, like elections, are presented.

5) Unfinished business, that is, motions being discussed when the last meeting adjourned, general orders, those motions that were postponed but not made into special orders, are presented again and discussed.

6) The assembly goes onto new business.

7) When the agenda is exhausted, then the meeting is adjourned.

There are various other possibilities that can be added to the agenda, such as an invocation of God or a deity, a flag procession and salute, announcements and roll call. To create a specific agenda, you will want to look at the previous meeting's minutes and search specifically for special orders and pending orders of business, otherwise known as unfinished business. You can also ask the members for agenda items to add to the agenda.

To adopt the agenda for a meeting, a vote is taken at the beginning of the meeting concerning the agenda. Some avoid adopting an agenda by vote due to the precious time it takes, which is a valid reason. However, one workaround is that the agenda may be mailed ahead of time to the members to vote upon at the beginning of the meeting. An invalid reason to not adopt the agenda by vote is for fear that the agenda cannot be amended. Indeed, it *can* be amended by a two-thirds vote of the membership.

Quorum

Quorum is the number of members that must be present, at minimum, for business to be conducted. If an order of business is adopted or if any decision is made by the assembly without the quorum present, the order will be null and void. This can happen at the beginning of the meeting or if members leave during the meeting.

Keeping a record of those present through roll call is generally a wise idea. This is doubly important, as a record of who is in attendance as well as a way of establishing that quorum was present.

If no quorum is present, there are four options. First, the presiding officer can initiate a short recess to gather members to obtain quorum. Second, the members can set a time and date to adjourn, that is, to resume the meeting. Third, the meeting can immediately adjourn, or dismiss. Fourth, the members can take measures to gather more members to establish quorum. Any of these, or a combination of these actions can be taken, but any other motion would be null and void without a quorum.

The Basics of Dealing in Motions

The way that business is presented and debated in a deliberative assembly according to Robert's Rules is that a motion is made to present an idea, and then the idea is discussed. The motion is made in the language, "Mr. President, I move to..." or "Madam President, I move that..." or some variation thereof. Then all the relevant information including who, what, when, where, and how are presented. This motion must be seconded to be discussed further. The presiding officer then restates the motion and asks for discussion, which occurs. Finally, the presiding chairman calls for a vote and announces the outcome of the vote as well as instructs who will carry out the motion should it be adopted.

In debating a motion, each member is given a turn to speak. The presenting member cannot speak against the motion, but other members may speak for or against, prefacing their comments with an indication of whether they support or disagree with the motion by saying, "I speak for the motion," or "I speak against the motion."

Taking a vote

The presiding officer realizes that it is time for a vote when no one stands to speak for or against the motion any longer. There are various types of votes, which we will discuss in a later chapter. If the motion passes, or "is carried," the president speaks that "the ayes have it," and if the motion fails, or "is lost," then the "noes have it."

If a member doubts the results of a vote, they may call out, "Division," without standing or being acknowledged first. This is the only time that it is acceptable to speak without being acknowledged first.

Resolutions

A resolution is a more formal motion, always written down and presented in written form. Occasionally, the resolution will contain a preamble which gives it context and tells the "why" in addition to the who, what, when, where, and how of the motion.

The Debate of a Motion

There exist parliamentary rules for debate to regulate for efficiency, fairness, and impartiality. There rules are as follows:

1) The presiding officer must recognize a member before he or she may speak, and the member must stand while speaking.

2) The member who presents a motion has the right to speak first about that motion once it have been seconded and presented for debate.

3) A member may speak up to two times concerning a motion, but their second turn is preceded by any who has yet to speak for the first time. That is, if anyone stands to speak at the same time as a person who would be speaking for the second time, the already spoken member must yield to the not yet spoken member.

4) Each member may speak for up to ten minutes unless the assembly otherwise specifies a different time limit.

5) What a member speaks about must be relevant to the motion and to the debate.

6) All remarks are addressed to the presiding officer and *never* to another member.

7) Respect and courtesy are required such that there will be allowed no profane language and no attacks on other members or questioning of motives.

8) Members refer to other members by titles and not by name, such as, "the delegate who just spoke" or "the representative of California."

9) Before presenting any information or argumentation for or against a motion, at the beginning of one's speech, a member will specify whether they speak for or against the motion.

10) The member who presented a motion may not then speak against the motion, though he or she may vote against it. The one who "seconds" the motion may speak for or against, and every other member may speak for or against.

11) A member cannot read long passages from a book or manuscript to support his or her point, but may repeat small, succinct, and relevant portions to drive their argument in debate.

12) A member cannot speak against or for changing a motion or action that is not pending unless that motion is up for debate, or unless he or she motions to amend, rescind, or reconsider such a motion.

13) As a courtesy, members should avoid whispering, and talking or walking across the floor during debate to avoid distractions to the discussion at hand.

14) The presiding officer sits down or stands back from the lectern when another member of the assembly is speaking to allow only one person to have the floor at a time.

15) If the presiding officer must correct the speaker on any point of parliamentary procedure or otherwise, should he or she need to interrupt the member, the member will sit down until the president completes his or her comments and then resume speaking.

16) Members may not give their leftover time to another member, but each speech is limited to ten minutes unless otherwise specified.

17) The presiding officer may not speak to an issue unless they give up their chair as the presiding officer to someone who has not spoken and does not wish to speak.

18) A member may conclude their debate with a higher-ranking motion than the one pending, something that will be discussed in a later chapter.

Voting Procedure

As with many things in parliamentary process, there is a proper procedure for taking a vote.

First, the chairman asks for the ayes, or those who affirm the motion and are in support of it.

Second, he or she will ask for the noes, or those who oppose it. The chairman will *not* ask for those who abstain, or for a count of those who do not vote.

The chairperson will then report the outcome of the vote and, should it be in the affirmative, will assign responsibility for carrying out the motion to an individual or group of members.

If the chairman is not certain of the outcome, he or she may ask for a rising vote, which we will learn about shortly. If a member questions the results, he or she will call out, "Division."

In all this, there are two crucial reminders: first, a quorum *must* be present to take a vote, else the decision is null and void. Also, the presiding officer must use language so that he or she is not taking a side in the debate. The proper wording would be, "those in favor" and "those opposed."

Types of Votes

The most common type of vote is the ***majority vote***. This only counts the number of ayes and noes. If 50 members are present, but only 40 of the members vote, only 21 are needed for a majority. More than half the number of total votes wins the vote in this case, and it does not include abstentions, the empty ballots.

On the other hand, there are two types of majority votes that are modified. The ***"majority of those present"*** requires that, in the case of 50 members present, 26 or more must vote aye or no to gain a majority vote to pass or be rejected. In this case, if 25 vote aye, 15 vote no, and 10 abstain, the motion still fails even though there were more ayes than noes, since the majority of those present did not vote in favor of the motion.

The ***"majority of the entire membership"*** vote requires, as it states, the majority of the entire membership to vote in favor or against a motion in order to pass or reject it. If quorum for your meetings of a 50-member organization is 26, and 26 are present at your meeting, all 26 would have to vote in favor of or against a motion in order to pass or reject it.

The ***two-thirds vote*** comes into play in certain circumstances like closing or limiting a debate, amending or suspending a rule previously adopted, taking away membership or office, and preventing the introduction of a motion. A two-thirds vote takes into consideration only the votes cast aye or no, that is, not the abstentions. Two-thirds of those voting must vote in either direction for a motion to pass or fail.

In some assemblies, a ***three-fourths vote*** is required in place of a two-thirds vote in certain circumstances, such as when the assembly is electing officers.

The ***tie vote*** occurs when fifty percent vote aye and fifty percent vote no, such that the count of cast ballots, excluding abstentions, counts half for and half opposed to a motion. This kills the motion because no majority can be found.

Methods of Voting

There are various methods of voting, of which the president can choose voting by voice, voting by rising or standing, voting by show of hands, or voting by general consent. The assembly may also take up a vote by ballot or by roll call, but they must vote to adopt this type of process for any particular motion. Once the vote is taken, the presiding officer calls out the results of the vote.

The first type of voting mentioned was the ***vote by voice***. The chairman speaks something to the effect of, "Those in favor say, 'aye.' Those opposed say, 'no.'" He or she will then judge by the number of voices on each side of the motion, whether for or against, which group was the majority and announce the results.

The second type of voting is the ***rising vote***, or the vote by standing. In this vote, the chairman uses the same language of "those in favor" and "those opposed," but instead of asking for a vocal response, he or she looks to the assemblymen to estimate how many are standing. The majority can be established this way as well.

The ***show of hands vote*** is, in turn, similar to the rising vote, but instead of standing, the delegates raise their right hands to establish their vote.

The ***vote by general consensus***, or vote by unanimous consent, is used for noncontroversial issues, like taking a recess, paying bills, and adjourning a meeting. It is not the same as a unanimous vote, but instead, the presiding officer will ask, "Is there any objection to...?" and the lack of objection will allow the passing of the motion. In these cases, it is not necessarily true that everyone consents, but that the objectors feel that opposing is useless and therefore do not voice their objection.

Taking a ***vote by ballot***, or a ballot vote, means that everyone can vote, including the president or chairman of the assembly. In this case, a ballot is given to each member of the assembly and then the ballots are placed in a ballot box. At some point the polls are closed and the votes are counted by a teller or tellers, and the chairman of the tellers' committee reads the results, at which point the presiding officer tells the outcome of the ballot vote.

Sometimes, ballot votes are taken by mail or by email as well. This is often the case for large or international organizations, or by organizations that cannot gather enough members at a time in one place to vote on an issue.

Taking a **vote by roll call**, that is, by gathering each person's vote one at a time, means that the vote is most accurate like the ballot vote, but also that it is no longer anonymous. The chairman cannot cast a vote in this type of process, but instead will tally the votes and tell the outcome of the vote.

Chapter 4: Motions in the Parliamentary Process

The motion is the driving force behind the parliamentary process: every decision and action is initiated by a motion. Having motions helps keep the assembly focused on one order of business at a time. This, in turn, promotes efficiency and clarity such that confusion over what is being discussed is not an issue.

There are five classes of motions:

1) Main Motions – part of the main group of motions

2) Subsidiary Motions – part of the secondary group of motions

3) Privileged Motions – part of the secondary group of motions

4) Incidental/Secondary Motions – part of the secondary group of motions

5) Motions that bring a question again before the assembly – part of the tertiary/third-ranked group of motions

Main Motions

Motions that introduce new business are the most common main motions. Main motions are made in the positive, such that if someone desires *not* to have something occur, they do not need to make a motion to that effect unless the body making that action is independent, such as a board beneath the assembly that might have the power to donate funds to various organizations.

The motion belongs to the presenter until it is repeated by the chairperson to the assembly. This means that the presenting member may change or alter the motion until the presiding officer presents it to the body, at which point the motion belongs to the body and must be dealt with accordingly.

Incidental main motions are motions that pertain to a main motion and do not bring up a new topic of discussion, but rather modify or clarify the main motion on the floor. These incidental main motions can do the following four things:

1) They can *ratify* the main motion. This means they can confirm an action without a quorum or make a decision that is dependent on a higher authority's approval.

2) They can move to *adopt* a main motion.

3) They can move to *limit* the amount of time spent on a main point.

4) They can move to *recess* and halt discussion for a short break.

Subsidiary Motions

There are a variety of subsidiary motions that can be taken in order of an established hierarchy. The lowest order of motion is the main motion, and only motions of higher order than the motion currently being discussed may be made. The following are the subsidiary motions in order from lowest to highest order.

Postpone indefinitely is the rank just above main motions in the hierarchy of motions, and its purpose is to kill the main motion during the meeting at hand without a vote. It must be seconded to be brought before the assembly. A majority vote is required to postpose indefinitely, and only a majority of ayes vote can be reconsidered. The result of this motion is that the main motion to which it pertains dies for the duration of the meeting.

The motion to ***amend*** the main motion is the next level up from postpone indefinitely. It also requires a second and can itself be amended. The majority must rule to amend a main motion before discussing it further, or else the main motion will continue in its original form. If adopted, the motion to amend will incorporate the change into the main motion that is pending and it will be considered by the assembly in its amended, rather than original, state.

Amending a motion might insert words into a motion, add words at the end of a motion, create a preamble to the motion, strike out words from a motion, or replace words in a motion. Only things that are relevant to the main motion or motion being amended may be brought before the deliberative body.

The motion to **refer to a committee** comes next in ascending the hierarchy of motions. The purpose is to have a smaller sub-group of the parliamentary assembly research and seek more information for the assembly to consider in debating the main motion. This also requires a second to be considered by the assembly as a whole. This decision requires a majority to be put into action, and its only debate is the merits of a committee rather than what the committee will consider. The motion then belongs to the committee to investigate rather than to the assembly until the committee reports back, or at the predetermined time that the committee was to report back.

A motion to **refer to the committee of the whole** or to **refer to the quasi-committee** is the motion to allow the assembly to consider the matter informally. This allows various members to speak as much as they desire and the decision or vote taken is simply seen as a recommendation by the committee rather than being considered the official vote. In groups of less than 50 members, this is called motion to **consider informally**. This type of motion needs a second and can be amended and debated. The majority vote is required to refer to the committee of the whole, and if it is adopted, the entire assembly begins to function as an informal committee rather than as a parliamentary body.

Another motion that can be adopted is the motion to **postpone to a certain time**. This allows the assembly to delay making a decision or put off the debate of a topic for a specific amount of time. This, again, requires a second. The amount of time that the decision-making process is being put off can be amended, should the assembly require it. The majority is required to adopt this subsidiary motion, and if it is adopted, the main motion is put off until later in the meeting or until the next meeting. If it is postponed until the next meeting, then it is brought to the assembly during the general orders and unfinished business segment of the meeting.

To **postpone to a certain time made into a special order** ensures that the main motion that is being postponed will indeed be taken up during the meeting at which it is specified to be taken up. This will also need a second and can be debated. The time at which the special order will be taken up can be amended at a later time as well. This *requires a two-thirds vote to adopt*. It will postpone until the date and time specified, but it *must* be taken up at that point, if for no other purpose than to postpone it again. It must be brought before the assembly for reconsideration should it be made into a special order.

The motion to **limit or extend the limits of debate**, if adopted, means that the rules of the debate will change, extending or shortening the accepted amount of time any one person may speak, increasing or decreasing the number of times the members may speak, or limiting the time within which the main motion may be discussed. This motion cannot be debated but must be voted upon immediately. It requires a second to be brought before the assembly for a vote. The element of time is amendable, and it takes a *two-thirds majority* to adopt.

There exists a higher order of motion, the motion to **close debate on the previous question**. When this motion is adopted, all debate on the main motion is halted and there is an immediate vote on the main motion. This cannot be debated or amended, and it requires a second to be considered by the assembly. *A two-thirds vote is required to adopt* this type of motion. This very high order motion is not appropriate in all cases, and in fact is inappropriate when not every member has had an opportunity to speak on an issue.

The highest order of subsidiary motion is the motion to **lay on the table**. This motion is *not* intended to kill a main motion or postpone a main motion, but simply to allow a more important or more urgent order of business to be brought before the assembly. This type of motion requires a second and cannot be amended or debated. It requires only a majority to adopt, but it cannot be reconsidered. If it is adopted, the main motion and all affiliated motions are set in the hands of the secretary to be taken up at a later time. This motion must be used sparingly or it will become abused.

Privileged Motions

The type of motion called a privileged motion is a motion that does not directly pertain to the order or motion at hand, but which nonetheless requires the attention of the assembly. These two have a hierarchy, such that only a higher order motion may be made when another privileged motion is being discussed, and the motions are resolved in order from highest to lowest in the hierarchy.

The lowest order privileged motion is called the **call for the orders of the day**. This can be called upon by one member and does *not* require a second. This motion is not amendable and not debatable. No vote is taken except a two-thirds majority needed to set aside the orders of the day. The purpose of this motion is to align the meeting with the agenda, such that the assembly will take up a general or special order. This motion, once adopted, stops what the assembly is doing and directs the meeting to proceed according to the agenda.

The next up in the hierarchy of privileged motions is the motion to **raise a question of privilege**. There are two types of questions of privilege: a question of the privilege of the assembly and a question of personal privilege. For example, the assembly might find the temperature too warm, or an individual might not be able to hear the member who is speaking. The presiding officer rules on these requests and as such does not require a second. It is not debatable.

The motion for **recess** is a privileged motion so that a short break may be initiated while business is pending without disrupting the flow of the parliamentary process. This motion requires a second and is not debatable, though the amount of time can be amended. It requires a simple majority to rule to adopt the recess, and it cannot be reconsidered. Its motion can be made again after an appropriate length of time, however. The purpose is to give the members and the officers a short break in the meeting.

There exists on the next step of the hierarchy the motion to *adjourn*. This ends the meeting immediately once it is adopted. It requires a second and is not amendable or debatable. Only a majority is required to adopt this type of motion. If it is not approved, the motion may be made again at a later time in the meeting. Any business or motions that are on the floor at the time of adjournment will be discussed in the next meeting when unfinished business and general orders are taken up.

When adjourning a meeting, it is sometimes necessary to *fix the time to which to adjourn*. This motion sets the times, place, and date at which the meeting will resume. It means that the meeting is not over but is suspended and will resume at the proper time and place. This is the highest order of privileged motions. It requires a second and the time and date of the adjourned meeting are amendable but not debatable. This type of motion requires a simple majority to approve.

Incidental Motions

Incidental motions do not have a hierarchy in the parliamentary process. They have no rank because they are addressed immediately in the process of deliberation.

A *point of order* is a motion taken to correct a breach of the rules or parliamentary order. There is no second necessary for this type of motion. It is not debatable and the presiding officer makes the ruling concerning the point of order, so no vote is taken.

If a member wants to disagree with the decision of the chair, they make a motion to *appeal*. This needs a second from the membership and is debatable but not amendable. The majority vote or a tie upholds the chairman's ruling on the issue.

As discussed earlier, a motion belongs to the issuer until the chairman repeats it for deliberation among the assembly. Once it is among the assembly, the issuer may make a motion to ***request for permission to withdraw or modify a motion***. The withdrawal does not need a second, while modification does require a second. The vote to withdraw is by general consent.

A member may also make a motion to ***request to be excused from a duty***. This requires a second if made by the individual and does not require a second if made by a member other than the individual being excused. This is amendable and debate is allowed, and it requires a majority vote, usually given by general consent.

The motion to ***object to consideration of a question*** prevents a main motion from being deliberated upon. No second is necessary and it is not debatable. Instead, a vote is taken and two-thirds must vote no to withdraw the motion from consideration.

A ***division of the assembly***, is a motion taken when the vote is in question, which requires no second and is not debatable, but instead a vote is taken immediately in a different form of voting than it was originally taken.

Division of the question, a motion to divide a main motion or amending motions into several separate motions, needs a second, is amendable but not debatable, and requires a majority vote. It cannot be reconsidered and, if accepted, this action separates the motion on the floor into a couple or several distinct motions to be considered separately.

The final incidental motion is the motion to ***suspend the rules***, such as to take up a topic out of order on the agenda or to suspend the rules of debate and vote immediately. This requires a second and is not debatable or amendable. It requires a two-thirds vote to suspend a rule or parliamentary order or the order of business, and to suspend a standing rule a majority is required. If adopted, the motion suspends, or sets aside, the rule in question and acts contrary to them.

Motions that Brings a Question Again Before the Assembly

This is a way that a member can bring a motion before the assembly again. The following motions return a question before the assembly for reconsideration.

One motion that can be put forward is to **take from the table** a motion that has been tabled. This requires a second and is not debatable. A majority rules on this motion. If it is adopted, the tabled motion becomes the pending business.

For the purpose of reviewing a motion that has already been passed or failed, there is the motion to **reconsider**. This type of motion can only be made by a member who voted on the winning side. It needs a second, is debatable, and requires a majority to adopt. It places the motion in question before the assembly again.

The motion to **rescind and amend something previously adopted** needs a second, is amendable and debatable, and requires either two-thirds vote or a majority of the entire membership, whichever is more practical. If adopted, this motion reverses or changes a previous motion that was formerly adopted.

A final motion that may be made in this category is the motion to **discharge a committee**. This takes the question and motion out of the hands of the committee and places it before the assembly, prior to the committee making its report. This needs a second, is amendable and debatable, and requires a two-thirds or majority of the membership vote, whichever is more practical, to adopt.

Now that we have looked at motions in depth, it is time to look at how membership works in the context of Robert's Rules.

Chapter 5: Roles within the Deliberative Body

There exist different roles of individuals within the assembly according to Robert's Rules. The subject of these roles is what we will learn about now. In a parliamentary assembly, the roles that exists are presiding officer, otherwise known as president, vice president, secretary, treasurer, board members, members of the assembly, and committee members. Having these roles present ensures the greatest level of efficiency, legitimacy, and fairness in the meeting that is being conducted.

President

The presiding officer might be elected from the membership or might come from outside the membership. The president's duties include the following:

1) He or she must **set goals for the organization** in some cases, such as in professional or business settings. The president will determine the goals and purpose of the organization and set the direction of the assembly's discussions as a result. This is the case for some assemblies, while in others the president is merely a presiding officer for deliberation.

2) The president **performs administrative duties**, such as signing legal documents, supervising employees, and speaking to the media as a representative of the organization.

3) He or she **presides at meetings**. The key roles of the presiding officer include to **keep order** by knowing and enforcing the rules of the parliamentary process, preparing the agenda ahead of time, coming to the meeting prepared to interact with motions by writing them down on

paper, calling the meeting to order in a timely fashion, and otherwise following the parliamentary process. The presiding officer **ensures fairness and impartiality** as part of his or her duties as well, such that the president may not enter debate or make motions, and he or she must aide members in phrasing their motions even if opposed to the motion. The chairman refers to himself or herself in the third person for the purpose of impartiality. Finally, as part of presiding at meetings, the president **protects the rights of the members**, such that he or she gently corrects a member for speaking out of turn or even speaks that a motion or delegate is acting out of order, which may be strong, accusatory language used in dire circumstances.

To be a good presiding officer, a person should have good judgement, be teachable and willing to learn, have and practice active listening skills, maintain calmness and peacefulness amidst stressful circumstances, be humble, and speak with firmness. They must weigh the costs of becoming the president of an assembly, as it will mean they are held to a higher ethical standard than the rest of the members.

The Vice President

The vice president is the one to preside over meetings. The vice president is referred to as Mr. or Madam President should he or she be taking on the role of the president, and should be called Mr. or Madam Vice President when the president is presiding. If the president's position is ever vacated, the vice president becomes the president.

There are some duties which only the president can accomplish, such as appointing members to committees, for example. This means that, even if the vice president is presiding, he or she will not be able to make those decisions.

Secretary

The secretary is responsible for a few duties. These are the following:

1) He or she must keep all the records of the organization together on file, including the reports of committees, and keep an updated list of the membership and member's names and information.

2) The secretary must notify members when they are elected to office or when they are appointed to a committee, providing them with all the proper documentation.

3) The secretary is responsible for giving notice to the members of an election or appointment that has been made of them to become a delegate at a convention. He or she will give them all the documents they then need.

4) He or she is the official signature on all the minutes and other certified acts of the assembly.

5) The secretary must maintain the bylaws, rules of order, standing rules, correspondence, minutes, and all other official documents of the organization and keep them updated.

6) The secretary informs the members by mail, email, or phone call of the approaching meetings.

7) The secretary takes minutes at all the meetings of the assembly, prepares the agenda with the president, and takes care of all correspondences. The secretary must know how to preside in case the president and vice president are not present, until the assembly chooses another chairman.

8) He or she is prepared by bringing a long list of materials to each meeting, including the minutes

book, a list of the bylaws, a list of the rules, the list of members, etc. etc.

The minutes are likely the most complex duty for which the secretary is responsible. A secretary familiar with the parliamentary process will better be able to record minutes because he or she will understand which motions are which, what to record, and what wording to use when recording pieces of deliberation.

The minutes are recorded in prose style, such that the document reads as a story of what actions were taken by the assembly, without the commentary of the secretary or of other members interspersed. The minutes are recorded by the secretary, formatted, read at the next meeting (and perhaps mailed ahead of time to the members for approval at the meeting), corrected if necessary, and finalized, at which point the secretary puts the approval date and his or her signature on the document, and files it with the rest of the minutes.

Every year, the minutes are gathered from the previous twelve months and bound on consecutive pages for official record keeping. This is also the secretary's duty and responsibility.

Treasurer

The treasurer is responsible for different duties in small and large organizations. In smaller organizations like small clubs, treasurer's duties include the following:

1) He or she receives and deposits the members' dues.

2) He or she gives receipts to the members for their dues.

3) The treasurer pays the bills that the assembly has voted to pay.

4) He or she gives reports at meetings about their activities.

5) The treasurer keeps records and prepares for the yearly audit.

6) He or she balances and reconciles the assembly's bank account.

In a larger organization, if there are employees, the treasurer is in charge of payroll. He or she files taxes. Therefore, a treasurer of a larger organization should be well aware of how to keep books and of accounting practices.

Resignations

Sometimes a person's personal life requires more of their attention, and they are unable to fulfill the duties of their office. In this case, it might be helpful to offer an assistant to help with time and work management.

Other times, a person resigns because of a basic disagreement with the organization or assembly. This should be addressed by looking at the communication patterns between members and with officers, such that you might find something that needs improvement. You can then address the issue.

Resignations should only be taken in writing, and should be submitted to the secretary only. Email resignations are not viable because they are not signed. Verbal resignations are not acceptable according to Robert's Rules. The resignation is then voted upon, and until the vote is taken, the officer can withdraw his or her resignation with no consequence.

Nominations of Officers

Nominations of officers for election can be done in a few ways, which follow:

1) There may be a **_nominating committee_**, preferably chosen by election of the membership or of the board. The nomination committee must inform the member that they would like to nominate him or her, and the individual must agree to nomination. Then, the nominations for each office are presented to the assembly to be voted upon. The nominations would fall under special orders in the order of business.

2) There might be **_nominations from the floor_** as well, especially in the case that the nominating committee is unable to find a willing person who is a best fit for the office being voted on. The nominator must know if the nominee would like to be nominated, and must refrain from nominating if the nominee is unwilling to serve in office. A person can nominate himself or herself, and no nomination requires a second. The president closes the nominations at the appropriate time and the elections are taken.

3) There might be **_nominations by ballot_**, in which the members vote by ballot and the tellers count the number of votes for each written name.

4) Nominations can be **_nominations by mail_**, especially in an international organization or in any other widespread organization.

5) The assembly might choose to do **_nominations by petition_**, in which the nominees must have a signed petition by the members behind them.

No matter what the case, the bylaws of the organizations will tell how the nomination process works and will instruct as to how to proceed in various situations.

Elections

Elections may be taken by various methods, but must be taken according to a method allowed by the bylaws. Some of the methods are as follows:

> 1) The first method by which a vote may be taken for an election is by **voice vote**. This is as it sounds, and is most useful when there is only one candidate for a position.
>
> 2) Another method for voting in an election is by **ballot vote**. There exist slated ballots with the candidates written in and a space for write-ins, which is a good idea for larger organizations. For smaller assemblies, each individual receives a ballot from the secretary, and the members each write the name of their chosen candidates.
>
> 3) Election by **roll call** is another method of voting, but loses the anonymity of the vote.
>
> 4) Electing a group of officers by **cumulative voting** is technically against the parliamentary process. It involves having a number of votes that you can cast for any number of candidates, and it means that you can cast more than one vote for the same person. This violates the democratic principle of one vote for one person. Nevertheless, some bylaws allow it and it is a method sometimes used for elections.

The tellers are the committee appointed to count and report the vote totals. The tellers should have a sheet on which they mark down each vote as they open it, should the vote be by ballot or other countable measurement.

Committees

Committees are the means by which most things are accomplished in assemblies. Committees can do anything asked of them, as long as allowed by the charter and bylaws of the assembly, or in other words, as long as the action is not out of order.

The bylaws will designate someone, usually the presiding officer, as the one to appoint committees and chairmen of committees. The secretary will inform and outfit the chairman and the committee members with whatever they need to accomplish their job.

There exist two types of committees. The **standing committee** is listed in the bylaws and is permanent to the organization. Members might change, but the committee itself remains intact. The standing committee receives its work regularly from the assembly or board, and then the chairman of the committee reports back about the accomplishment of the task.

The **special committee** is formed for a specific, short-term or limited task. This is also called a select or ad hoc committee. The two roles a special committee might have would be to investigate further into an issue and report back the findings to the assembly, making a recommendation at times as to how to proceed. The other purpose of the special committee is to implement a resolution or adopted motion, and report back to the assembly once the deed is accomplished and the motion has been carried out to completion.

The chairman of the committee acts as a presiding officer of sorts, though in a much less formal manner. He or she will speak for the committee and preside over the committee as long as he or she possesses the office of chairman. Most often, the chairman is chosen by the presiding officer over the deliberative body.

Members' Role

The duties of the membership and of each member are as follows:

> 1) The members should arrive on time to meetings, be prepared by reviewing the proper information

ahead of time, be familiar with parliamentary rules, and most of all, attend meetings regularly.

2) A member should always prepare for leadership: one never knows when he or she will be appointed to a leadership role in a committee or be nominated for leadership office.

3) Members need to accept assignments to committees and carry out the assigned duties in a timely fashion.

4) Members need to work with each other in harmony despite occasional disagreement.

5) When voting in the minority or losing side, a member must remember that majority rules and gracefully submit to what the majority has spoken.

6) Members need to be fair, respectful, and impartial as the president is, such that they do not use the parliamentary rules, such as calling a point of order, unless absolutely necessary and never to sway the membership to their side of an issue.

7) When something has gone awry and the bylaws or other rules are being violated during a meeting or outside a meeting, the members each have a responsibility to bring attention to the violation.

Unruly Members and Discipline

There are various steps that may be taken when a member or officer are acting in an unruly manner during a meeting.

First, the presiding officer can **call the member to order**, not naming them but simply referring to the individual as "the member."

Next, the chair can **name the offender**, calling him or her out by name and giving specifics of their offense. This is done in second person, directly addressing the member in a humble but firm tone.

Third, there are penalties that may be imposed for unruly behavior. They include the following, in order of least to most severe:

1) The membership might adopt a motion that the offending member must apologize.

2) The motion might be adopted that the member must leave for what is left of the meeting and cannot return until the next meeting.

3) A motion might be made to censure the member, that is, to warn them that further misbehavior will lead to being suspended or expelled.

4) The membership might agree that the offending member must be suspended for a specific amount of time from their rights as a member.

5) The most severe is the motion to expel the member from the assembly and withdraw all rights as a member permanently.

If an officer is censured and then is up for suspension or expulsion, a trial must be held to determine the outcome.

Chapter 6: Meetings

There exists more than one type of meeting according to the parliamentary law of Robert's Rules. All meetings require a quorum to be present for any business to be considered. Every type of meeting has a presiding officer or someone who is leading the meeting as well as someone who is taking the minutes. These meetings must be announced ahead of time to all members, including the date, time, and location.

Formal Meetings

The first type of formal meeting that we will discuss is the **annual meeting**. This type of meeting either means that the assembly only meets once a year *or* that the assembly has an annual meeting required by its bylaws. Business from the second type of annual meeting can be carried over to the next regular meeting if it becomes unfinished business.

Regular meetings happen at regular intervals and are specified in the bylaws stating the day or interval of the meetings. The standing rules will designate the hour of the meeting. Business can be carried over by postponing to the next meeting, referring a motion to a committee, laying a motion on the table, and reconsidering a motion if the meetings are at least quarterly. Otherwise they can only be carried to the next session by referring to a committee.

Adjourned meetings are technically an official continuation of a previous regular or special meeting. At the beginning to an adjourned meeting, the minutes of the meeting being continued are read and then business continues as though there has been no break in the process.

There is another type of meeting called an **executive session** in which the members are the only ones allowed to be present at the meeting. Ordinarily a member can bring a guest to a meeting, but in executive session the guests are disallowed from being present. The purpose is to conduct business without the watching eyes of outsiders, such as when disciplinary action is being taken against a member.

A ***special meeting*** is also known as a "called meeting" and is held at a different time than the regular meeting. Bylaws must allow for special meetings or they cannot be held. These meetings concern a specific subject of deliberation and are restricted to discussing that subject.

Sessions are a succession of meetings dedicated to dealing with a specific order of business, or program of business. Conventions often use sessions to connect a series of meetings.

In a ***convention***, delegates are chosen to represent groups of people who are scattered geographically, and each delegate represents their own unit of the organization. Rather than calling every member together, delegates represent groups of members. A committee creates standing rules for the convention that differ oftentimes from the parliamentary law governing regular and special meetings.

A ***mass meeting*** is a meeting of an unorganized group that has not adopted parliamentary law or any other organizing principles. Because of this, the sponsoring parties have the right to govern as they would like.

Informal Meetings

Informal rules for meetings are meant for groups with less than twelve members.

Board meetings with less than twelve members can be more relaxed in their procedures. They do not need to stand when speaking and can speak more than twice or any number of times they would like. There is no need for seconds in an informal board meeting. The chairman can make motions and discuss just as any other member in an informal meeting as well.

Committee meetings are another meeting type that often consists of less than twelve members, and thus it has informal rules as well. The chairman is very active in this type of meeting and makes motions and debates just as much as the other members, if not more. The chairman will often act as the secretary as well, taking down the minutes. Committees do not make decisions, per se, but make recommendations to the assembly and give information to the assembly that they have discovered or discussed.

Chapter 7: How to Begin Using Robert's Rules

Now that you have a more in-depth understanding of how Robert's Rules function, you might desire to start using them in your meetings at work in a business context, in your volunteer work as part of a nonprofit board of directors, in your gardening club, for your next family reunion, in your fraternity or sorority meetings, or in many other contexts. The question remains though: how? This chapter will give you a launching point from which to start implementing Robert's Rules in various areas of your life.

Learn

Read as much as you can about Robert's Rules so that you can learn as much as you can about the Rules and how they work. Read through this book over and over, and read other materials in print and online about Robert's Rules. You will want to have a copy of *Robert's Rules of Order* in your meetings once you start using them, so buy a copy and have it with you whenever you enter a meeting.

The more you learn about Robert's Rules, the more you will be comfortable with them. The more comfortable you are with them, the more persuasive you will be in adopting Robert's Rules for your meetings, family reunions, sorority or fraternity decision-making sessions, or any other meeting you or assembly of which you might be a member.

Propose

Propose to your group that you adopt Robert's Rules as your parliamentary law. Make sure that your charter and bylaws allow for such an adoption. If it is allowable, propose to the group and give reasons as to why Robert's Rules would benefit them and the group as a whole.

Educate

Educate the group about Robert's Rules, recommending them this book and others that will help them to understand Robert's Rules of parliamentary law. Tell them why you want to adopt the rules and what benefits you see. Be as specific as possible. Focus on how Robert's Rules will increase the following:

1) First, they will increase *efficiency* of meetings, helping you to get through a long list of subjects or a long agenda without the hiccups of wondering what will happen next. The agenda and the policy of having one main motion on the floor will aide this goal, eliminating confusion and increasing the smoothness of the meeting.

2) Robert's Rules promote the *legitimacy* of a gathering by having a secretary recording minutes, and having an official record of the work done in a meeting. Instead of a free-for-all without any direction, the meeting has a presiding officer who ensures that the fairness and efficiency of the meeting are not compromised in the process of debate.

3) In addition, using Robert's Rules will ensure the *fairness* of a meeting and the democratic process will be certain to reign in the assembly if Robert's Rules are adopted. No single individual's vote matters more than another's, and the impartiality of the presiding officer helps make sure that both the majority and minority voices are heard, though the majority rules in any decision.

4) If you have a large organization or an organization that is spread out, adopting Robert's Rules will create a *uniformity* of process, such that each smaller piece of the whole organization will accomplish business in the same way as any other branch of the organization. For example, 4H clubs, Boy and Girl Scouts, national fraternities and sororities, and many other organizations can

benefit from Robert's Rules' unifying nature, and when one member visits another segment of the same organization, they will be familiar with the process and easily integrate into deliberation along with the other members.

5) Robert's Rules can help increase the ***competence*** of the members as well as of the officers and president of an assembly to make decisions. Knowing and abiding by these rules as parliamentary law will give the assembly a structure within which it can work. This means that, instead of fumbling around for a way of doing things, the entire assembly is agreed on a process and knows what to expect and when things are out of line. Setting up the members' and officers' expectations is extremely important in any meeting.

Vote

The democratic process is quintessential to parliamentary law, so if you are going to adopt Robert's Rules, you need to have the majority vote for their adoption. You cannot impose these rules on the assembly as a presiding officer or otherwise, as this would cause the process to be something other than democratic.

You can, however, offer Robert's Rules as bylaws to govern a deliberative body, and, should you oversee the assembly, you can write and customize the rules to your parliamentary body's purposes, but the assembly must vote to adopt the rules as written. Only then will Robert's Rules be the legitimate ruling force behind your process.

Implementing Robert's Rules

Once the rules are adopted, each person, both officers and members, needs to be furnished with a means of understanding

Robert's Rules and a copy of the bylaws. An important resource is the actual book, the Eleventh Edition called *Robert's Rules of Order, Newly Revised*. Providing this to the members will help them to understand the rules by which they must function, and it keeps them accountable to abiding by the rules.

This book that you are reading is another great resource to help members interpret *Robert's Rules of Order*, such that any confusion over the language in *Robert's Rules* can be made understandable by knowing the principles explained in this book.

The bylaws must be made available to each member and officer as well, as this is how they will be able to ensure that their motions and actions are lawful according to the rules of order established in the bylaws.

Getting Informal (and Practical)

Not everything about an assembly governed by Robert's Rules needs to be as formal as outlined in this book. It is better to start out formal, though, and to relax as time goes on than to try to increase formality later.

It might be that your assembly is a group of businessmen: especially if there are less than twelve members, relax the rules as outlined in the section on informal meetings.

In larger meetings, it is better to have Robert's Rules more formally established and to abide by them more closely. This will help ensure the fairness, expediency, and competence of the meeting.

Practice

Practice will go a long way in learning and abiding by the parliamentary law put forward in *Robert's Rules of Order*. The more you use Robert's rules, the more familiar you will become with them, and the easier it will be to recall the next time you need to know how to proceed in a specific situation.

Conclusion

Thanks again for taking the time to read this book!

You should now have a good understanding of Robert's Rules of Order, and how to implement them in an organization of your choosing!

If you enjoyed this book, please take the time to leave me a review on Amazon. I appreciate your honest feedback, and it really helps me to continue producing high quality books.

www.ingramcontent.com/pod-product-compliance
Lightning Source LLC
Chambersburg PA
CBHW061100050726
47592CB00004B/1764